D0104775

Also by Aaron Shurin

A Door
The Paradise of Forms: Selected Poems
Unbound: A Book of AIDS
Codex
Into Distances
Narrativity
A's Dream
Elsewhere
The Graces
Giving up the Ghost
Toot Suite
The Night Sun
Woman on Fire

for Jane

INVOLUNTARY LYRICS

for

Aaron Shurin

in Austin

March 2006

INVOLUNTARY LYRICS

AARON SHURIN

OMNIDAWN
RICHMOND, CALIFORNIA
2005

Front and back cover: Bust 2, 1998, 'China.China' series by Ah Xian.
Porcelain body cast with handpainted underglaze blue landscape design.
Approximately 30 x 20 x 41.5 centimeters. Made in Sydney, Australia.
Images by Ah Xian courtesy of Queensland Art Gallery, Brisbane, Australia.

Book cover and interior design by Ken Keegan.

Offset printed in the United States of America
on archival, acid-free recycled paper
by Thomson-Shore, Inc, Dexter, Michigan.

Library of Congress Catalog-in-Publication Data
appears at the end of the book.

OMNIDAWN®

Published by Omnidawn Publishing
Richmond, California.
www.omnidawn.com
(800) 792-4957

ISBN-13: 978-1-890650-23-0
ISBN-10: 1-890650-23-4

9 8 7 6 5 4 3 2 1

Grateful acknowledgement is given to the following books and journals in which some of these poems first appeared:

Boo, Court Green, Electronic Poetry Review, Fourteen Hills, The Germ, Interim, LIT, Loghost, Lyric &, mark(s), New American Writing, Onyx, Parthenon West, Raddlemoon, Remap, syllogism, Traverse, Volt, Zyzzyva;

The Paradise of Forms: Selected Poems (Talisman House, 1999), *Word of Mouth: An Anthology of Gay American Poetry* (Talisman House, 2000), *The Blind See Only This World: Poems for John Weiners* (Granary Books/Pressed Wafer, 2000).

The author wishes to express his appreciation to many assiduous friends and readers who maintained active interest in this work, and to the artist Ah Xian, whose sculptural fusions chime, heal time, and rouse the vale of soulmaking.

CONTENTS

Which eyes not yet created shall o'erread

William Shakespeare

I.

If the judgment's cruel
that's a wake-up call: increase
energy, *attention*. These little pumpkins ornament
themselves with swells, die
pushing live volume packed spring-
form hard as a knock: Decease
and resist. Content
surges exactly as memory
closes its rear-guarding
eyes
— the world rushes *in* not *by*! just be
steady, receptors, measure is fuel:
whatever moves move with the
drift which moving never lies.

II.

Kim Novak's in *Vertigo* Kabuki slash of eyebrow
permanent command up praise
on open field,
alarmed canvas indicative this way eye no use
resisting mask of that intention; remembered now
as if perfect attitude were a brow of mine —
or had he held
stronger or longer could it then excuse
the shadow lies
underline
my eyes for days?
No, no problem, nothing counts for old
when opening lyric eyes
raise havoc and fire the cold.

III.

San Francisco, ah, west
of ascension, none of us wanted posterity
before we got to pleasure it! Another
sick, sickening, the
last newest
in his prime.
You, for all of us came crawling through dim alleys to mother
and shining see
even if still we're trailing in and out of city's womb
calls us and too discharges time
alone inside our tender bodies — dry,
do, my still-seeing eyes; nightmare's made me raise my fearful head
again. Be
extravagant meaningful polis, clearful sky, the
really it has been loving gesture of light undoes the tomb!

V.

Various frame
where
inside dwell
what outside left
but permeable, the same.
She made her heart of glass
woundingly if broken movingly if met, excel
where transparency is valued for truth, bereft
of solidity inflexible, on
view. That was
a dream we shared so she was there
to meet
me but I, I, I was gone
to find a man, couldn't then tell her, *this was long ago*, a man, many,
        so sweet.

VI.

one
might thrill notes deface
progression level notice art
distilled
syncopate the
order here or there's in place
on landing or air arrive depart
means self killed
that governor bereft of posterity
yay! and ego's usury
of event modality fair
shifts whoever I was on loan
for using using me the
beat up drummed on drummed up time keeper, loser, error, heir

VII.

Everyone around's having 50th birthdays, pilgrimage
markers, up in Bodega Bay light
grayed above cliff face, distant seals' bark, so far yet so clear, car
of evening riding in with billowing cape: another metaphor for age?
      Oy! The eye
that should have met mine didn't, reversed from that day
troubles friendship subterranean unspoken such complications, sight
uneasy forward from backward lit, are
we then in this stupid majesty
both lost and found or in *and* out or on *and* off our way?
On the hill
with moon-pod wild thistles, shaggy, noon
seeming midnight in their spooky glare, we met, climbing, three age-
marked walkers, 70s I guess, caustic, bright, two women pals and
      gentleman poet. I might've been son.
The throaty ducks shut up, we introduced, locked eyes, really there
      is mutual pleasure, wind-silvery eucalyptus leaves and their
      pentagram nuts suspended, still.

VIII.

I come to cafe, I sit, I bear
my part in the general cruise. One, sadly
won't look at me, another
won't look away; ridiculous assumption and snarled consumer joy
in abeyance, ordering
quotidian life according to compulsions or ordered *by*, focus shifting
        but always aligned. Well, gladly
I'd mother
that guy with a stubble but he wants a father. I won't annoy
his diligent linearity. Man I just yesterday had sex with in park
        — sing
muse — said "Yum" and somehow knew to pull my head on his
        shoulder, little bleating sounds.
One heart, one mind, one chance but right now one
second's second chance he just walked by this cafe walkman in ear
real time I could've run and, what, left the poem? Composition
        deems none
such interruption permissible; shit, the sheer complexity confounds.

XI.

Away

from yellowed leaf, November, in park bench solitude, across where
      bright grass, *late November!* still grow

a man, face to sun, looks hundred yards through window at me who
      store

his traces within the gesture of this lengthening line. He'll depart

(he did), perish

from chanced to bestow

on me and I on him. Yesterday a heroin dealer nailed beneath
      window by cops more

numerous at least than he, convert

and reveal an impostor hippy, they scorned, into a predatory freak,
      they high-fived. Then the homeless woman with permanent
      porch to cherish

two doors down, clothing stuffed behind bushes, howled in night
      increase

rage and volume against who sneakily was occupying her slim
      though regular berth. Thereby

decay

became a part of my impossible sleep: I saw the unlikely son of
      Diane di Prima and Woody Allen die

own hand because, it seems, inside the dream he kissed me
      repeatedly, eleven years old, and wanted more; refused. Then
      what desire was forced to sleep and cease?

XIV.

Diction is lexicon to find
as from strung pluck
what airs, derive
interconstellate concentric an astronomy
of lines then lines art
with luck
indeterminate solipsism thrive
as harmony even ugly sound quality
give sanctity to colloquy by which convert
monologue to tell
them so prognosticate
wind
coming in this date
news well

XVI.

Beloved counterfeit
self in the way
of monotheism repair
a rupture in time
so that duplicity is multi pen
this way against it the face decay
from hair so lovely to fair
complexion wants to be crushed only rhyme
stand men on men
for hours
still
made set
the glance from gardener's skill
raise virtual flowers

XVII.

Go turn away baby faces
who've come
wailing to deride age
the sumptuous desserts
on pliable tongue
sweeten veering tomb
with syrup of rage
Several parts
on a breeze dispersal are song
for closing eyes
envisioned by slow time
How weary as fluffy graces
drift intravenous pile rhyme
on downy head where sleeping lies

XVIII.

Those guys with Christmas tree untrimmed
and me to help, nobody else came, party day
fade
away unless I hang 'em. So here's my faux-pearl earring and necklace
    set, temperate
compared to some, countering your scary Guatemalan death-squad
    burnt angel. But owe
me no thanks this shimmying electric May-
pole brightens December shade.
X didn't call me for a date
though I foisted number on him after severe flirtations, what he
    might grow
in proportion to those giant feet shines
elsewhere, someone else'll see
it. Still I've no complaint, except employment chances dimmed
but that's perennial this annual, the
season's one for newing, I'm drinking, it's raining, I saw a plum
    blossom lone bluey pink on live branch for which tired
    December declines.

XIX.

Job's a crime
for security like I've seen too much *Wild America* on PBS, vicious
       eats vicious necessity, paws
spring claws, lower prognathism managers with brow
slanted brood-
ing. It's such economy of necessity makes clear this pen
surrounded by jaws
gaping allow
little blood
to reach us pups — ah, men
you power fucks fleet's
not fast enough to outrun your wrong
even if cheetah OK too much TV time
makes me too young
if not foolish with false simile still it'd be nice not to mention fair to
       taste some of them sweets. . . .

XXI.

knit purl hems
lined turned to muse
on finish as if write
verse
to be *in* verse fair
weather of *being in measure* use
body to pulse bright
keening syntactic or it uses corpus rehearse
is all performance air
guitar compare
well
as ultra lyre rail or purr for gems
deific sonic parts string unity sell
plurality convergence anywhere rare

XXIV.

the eyes
of cruising Dante named threading, stellar
compass to pass this way have done
with me or you, heart
warming literal your hands on me
held
sun
so art-
fully the
skill
employed rub down heat from on high art
hand lies
over heart
contain clamorous overbeating still

XXV.

Friendships die
as passions do or AIDS took 'em, the stars
those florid queens who might've danced tabletop at X-mas party
        lost fight
though we inhabit periphery, tamed if not undone, gaze empty
        dance floor, no boast.
Nobody foiled
but nobody won, bars
filled with younger-than-me's filled with visions not quite
possible, though most
released at least from toiled
through unloveliness unloved. Mahmoud and Ahmed proprietors
        put out spread
of dips and crudités flavored beer but my dearest beloved
dolls, though *un*ghostly companions right and left seated, to my
        spectral eye
were all removed
big open cafe floor unpeopled gone and buried. . . .

XXVI.

The face of it
unnamed devotion vassal
not moving
except keeling where knit
to floor in vacant aspect
of glorious sage
some specious dream of loving
without wit
to save respect
comes up from eyeing you, cold-blues, the fool is mine
before yours abject the
piece of it
unnamed long ago taken from me
that I say "you" wanting "mine"

XXVIII.

If friends gather in the
lamp light
their eyes — *those* friends — hatch bright
flickers like zap guns and catch you. You know. Rest
in that assurance as if heaven
were a new boyfriend of night.
Dearest night
sweat-slick with dark hair patterns oh pressed
on my template eyes on eyes of every kind make even
weight of forward and backward motion, reign
gyroscopic the longer
for his spraying warm cum on me.
The look he gave me swept night inside stronger
for his holes in the dark — those stars — simple piercing plain.

XXX.

every functional sight
marries possible thought
reach conclusions foregone
and foretold seconds past
firsts made over
tones reached sought
as nexus vital moan
not want nor have no waste
after if not taken before
has each false stop in flow
a friend
elision twilight pushes or pulls night
inside of joie de jour or out of woe
ends neither start nor end

XXXII.

love men
all day
in thought
pull cover
from age
make survey
inventory brought
to lover
body's equipage
suck time
panoply prove
inside pen
mutual love
rhyme rhyme

XXXIII.

Freaking out's no disgrace
like I saw last night self seen
as other, just the outsideness freaks. Used to it from years of
        marijuana; shine
startled eye
no matter brow
will edge the too green
with proportioning shade. Six hours of passion unleashed mine
on his after the fact, out of control, but that was other me, alchemy
of routine substance fused toward riskier flight. Now
I see predilections compulsive but, well, kindly; ride
permutations without disdain
to meet another face
of mine. Such temporary stain
wash out easy morning when — hey —nothing-to-hide.

XXXIV.

She find no disgrace
eating marriage by day,
image orbit, blood orbit, grief's
the language cloak
tied shut. Inside dark effulgent loss
swirls open way;
outside — "he wore a tan coat" — cuts figure in relief,
fixed smoke.
Would cross
not over but through and back is break
hold, sheds
inextinguishable name, inviolate face,
invaluable deeds.
Autumn and silk and nothingness speak.

XXXV.

sex for Shakespeare tech are
smell fingers struggle for balance being sucked-off vertical musical
       spring done
professional with harmonic sense
dragging hem happily in mud
provocative declension advocate
equilibration by hair or spit sun
dried by mind light really juice vamp with lexical wig commence
turning bud
void of shame so sans hate
wordily fleurs this
vibraphone pollinated behind be
bone on bone together compare
an anybody range of gestures phrases reactions arriving me
all target swollen hit or miss

XXXVII.

It's a country road forty years ago, a country store
where propped outside, banded tans and gold, are sugar cane several
      feet's delight
taller than especially me, despised
outsider New Yorker in temporary captive preadolescent Texas
      youth,
stymied circumspect narrowed to hold it in mouth, give
pleasure like dog with bone chewing and sucking to spite
poverty East Texas limitless, oh, nothing, stupid pleasure sufficed.
Stupid pleasure suffices? Shop spend decorate mad for eye view
      prowl sex get it or don't eat truth's
live
with stuffing it. Dad(dead)'s right here to watch. That fucker had wit
but no brain rage but no heart figure but no beauty the
knowing failure terror of him lies in wait fifty years and more
but I've dealt with him! I've dealt with him! though he with me
ghostly not finished, patiently hides to seek, smiling, sit and wait,
      wait and sit. . . .

XLI.

On my log perch in the park — finally sun prevailed
after weeks of rain — commits
one's eyes to color, a certain sheen, bare
before light or clothed in light, heart-
shaped clover fluffs up, dew drops play globe, stinky acacia's
       blooming youth-
like glandular smell befits
a day seems young, randy even, turning it toward luscious age — so
       there
in vivid distance one sees Mt. Diablo as attainable, San Francisco
       itself a perch or point of view, high art's
mental cartography, plum blossoms pinking the air. Truth
won
for clear light a city diversity grandeur cliff's edge the
giddy flight over moaty Bay or endless imagination Pacific assailed
by wave froth and fog dramatic but *not* veiled so pure Northern
       light prevails, "true" visual light on me
now right side cleared and raised in heat besotted devoted son.

XLII.

remounted the bright stair by being remounted in her
attention, plum blossoms white as well as pink I discovered, whiter
      than grief's
mere sustenance. Saxophone mellows a bass in Benny Carter's
      mouth, gain
for my ears clearly
synchronous, one year ago surprised in bold February sun the heave
      of air sucking up loss
from AIDS encoded as storm-ravaged trees, now second February
      here sun again is chief
instigator leveling by heat two
in a row undoes projection, I'd forgotten plums exploded early then,
      too. Nearly
ready now to beach early spring across
the gray sand leading pools of footprints you
punch a momentary path then vanish in late light one
needn't depend on skin or bones, easy incarnation, beside her
passing father simultaneous a child alone
or you waving bye to me from where you're coming toward me

XLIII.

The difficulties are so
alluring where cigarette butt, peony, the glass sphere, and prostate
       don't actually meet. See
the man who's wrapped himself in shirred gold — he *made*
that outfit! A pasta dish including vegetables gets respected
while a flying line of brown pelicans haul tide. The day
is longer than 24 hours given what we remember, a feature and *its*
       features. The
shade
we wanted fell across sun's face a map of Northwest states or
       somebody's dream of north directed
up. Let's stay
focused on the bright
shadow of noon with its google eyes, the
"golden weight of attention." A person is hungry under the plane
       tree, says "Show
me
your pure function among objects give me a light."

XLIV.

"Be
not afraid of my body," thought
Whitman as if beating down his own thought
swollen with hesitation in the way
of pleasure. The heaven of body was gone
to thought's heaven. "I brought
my own self to the headlands" he wrote post climax solo wrought
of projections in language where hands didn't have to stay
put the book he squeezed let out a moan
close to his chest where a gray hair got stuck in its uncut pages. I
    take a stand
on my knees to favor his slow
leak into the future where books squeeze back this time in your
    arms the writing's on me *"the*
body of this thought must be a star" if it tingles, zoom heavenly body
    searing woe-
filled with chaos burning toward — woo! — trembling anticipation
    of the wet land.

XLV.

Pester melancholy
rigor, fire
neurons disposition syntactic recured
as chains hung tensile "de clocher à clocher . . . d'étoile à étoile",
      singular objects bye-byed
on strung chords the
pure fibrillations desire
tines struck times a concourse assured
of overload rise and slide
as if pumped semantic were a fat load of me
gone
overboard or towers penetrated by sky dunk roses in brine glad
shivers the
torque might unfashion discrete sad
monosyllables with no context or poor context alone

XLVII.

plays another part
who took
another look at "love"
as it appeared shameless in an other
poet's poem. me:
don't look
move
over you're smother-
ing the
feast.
he: lines of sight
raised from paper where "heart"
is raised shameless delight
invite in and saturate the guest

XLVIII.

thief
all way
beat chest
thrust
chin pose art
big make stay
beat breast
what trust?
rip apart
are
you in fear
or grief
mon dear
form care

LI.

Dear *leptospermum,* tiny magenta flowers on needly branches, please
    know
I meant no offense
mistakenly conflating you with AIDS-related intestinal disorder
    cryptosporidium — the pace
of vocabulary assimilation is mocked by speed
of exfoliating information dropped in saturated brain. I know well
    your floral twinkle made
of sober contrast and mistook you in name only; raise, then,
your superior modesty my way again, please. In race
last night to spy through window at street disturbance nervous need
proved careless I broke favorite yellow vase with rain-like slashes on
    it jaded
in my hurry to control, find
out the source of someone else's noise. You hearty desert flower slow
down my attention as you must slow
infrequent rain, I'll go
absorbed more cautiously your small determined face in blustery
    wind

LII.

bird   net

sweet pea   skeleton   key

knock   chest

fog   green   treasure

vibrate   h-ome   hide

back-of-knee   19th C cinema   survey

path loop   fearless rhyme   blessed

receptor   pleasure

technique   à main   pride

fold   still meaning   in stillness   inflection   rare

"nearer to heaven"   belly   scope

radio tube   portable   set

genital mirage   salvo   diaristic hope

where   history   are

for Allen Ginsberg

LIII.

even death is new
what he made of you made
you enliven in me this year
of your last will be all yours Whitman said "these tend
outward to you" nakedness is in my eye show
hairy belly shameless like you used to, shade;
appear
without fear lend
exuberance to shame-faced, faces to faceless don't know
true visage or as you said "the self as lovely" Allen counterfeit
of Allen the real who's here in pages why wholer in death I can see
      you better part-
ing mists to reveal *work* while you
float roly-poly on heart-
shaped cloud giddy sad with Aeolian harmonium ready, set

for Allen Ginsberg

LIV.

rupture discloses
space "buried coherence" those trunks & who we are of them seem
there but there's more show
finer trunks call roots give
all as fade
from view deems
not seen not there so
skillfully weave dizzy up down spring live
though San Francisco can't cough-up frozen clod made
anyway pink tulip tree plum blossom *leptospermum* blush dye
city sign youth
sigil roses
for blistering i.e. blossoming truth
over and over only

LV.

waking up gastric into memory
of who I betrayed lying monuments
to — what? — enmity
against — what? self? father? — why dream now not really dream
          but rhyme
psychic disposition to unfocused other room
peopled spewing contents
of — what? — locked in brain posterity
replay diminishes time
mobius mirror doom
same view over same view overturn
not "mine" but structures of interplay arise
doubled self as other or other as self such masonry
behind eyes
looking at — what?— make eyes burn

LIX.

A man's (sic) just a shell enclosing a pulsating tooth; mine abscessed
       is done
governing me, is
gone, a hole. Say
I'm beguiled
by that frame
of nothingness, *not* a hole *a gum* yet "tooth" still rules searching
       tongue, a miss
more active than a hit. Proust-body that parts maintain the parts they
were a child
holding tooth in hand the same man contemplates a dream of
       pillow, the same
contract with pain, the same open look.
Then let me sleep for days
or a life, sun
on my face upraise-
d a shell surrounding a hole, a tooth in a book

LXI.

Black cat wakes to jealousy
over big crow's open
transport, tougher muscles, great
punctuating beak, night
of feathers. Stays awake
licking broken
pride, springs halfheartedly toward moth defeat
in its retracted claws, losing sight
of murderous crow. For whose happy sake
do ugly mouthy crow's wings beat, the
paragon of elsewhere
to pry
back the close air in neat
finishing strokes? Me.

LXII.

Sun surmount
fog an overpowering eye
forcing sight as deed
so sky *really* part
and hale us with this gesture of antiquity:
clearing noon. A remedy
of stilled space is read
into the logbook of the day. Old friend (former lover I thought
       AIDS-dead) you speak of "heart"
like anyone would know it as a *space* come into — long ago iniquity
of city sludge long ago — here in river country redwood silent your
       happily clear eyes on — no *in* — mine
while offer me an endless spiel Native American sweatlodge (you're
       Italian!) apocalyptic Egyptian pyramidal (oy!) doom and
       fervent praise
though twinkling, too, (if grandiose) account
of five years' — sweet-natured and *still alive!* — intervening days
settle processional downstream and substance of time define. . . .

LXIII.

spring
now
& fortify
overworn
syntax *sentences*, oof, lyric knife
to brow
excise memory
i.e. what comes before or after false whole morn-
ing's total life
each time or night
is when seen
exactly king
never prince first green
bud forget flower for sight

LXIV.

Store
defaced
face "inside," a state
of raw sensate — *rubbed* raw — age
can't hide with decoy
wrinkles, folds. If I were razed
from this elder-ness altitude, ruminate
true to my rage
— raw-faced — on what let get away
could I gain
at least connective tissue anchor that dissolve to this fixedness and
      choose
again . . . ? Men on every shore,
waving me back forgiving from my middle course I lose
another face each time I won't remember to remain.

*Freight boat smell of rectal mucus went down off England with all dawn
smell of distant fingers. . . .*

William Burroughs

LXV.

It decays
  — *I* do — in me & on me — a sea
change for lack
of power
to alter what it hid:
hurtling toward death. "Your plea,
Madame, has been sent back."
Flower
then fall. They're all around me, departed, having been ghosted and
        forbid
any other return. The sun's out.
It might
shine for days.
It shines for days relentless bright
as their cold vagrant eyes — *mine from the start!*

*That heart pulsing in the sun and my cock pulsed right with it and jism seeped
through my thin cotton trousers and fell in the dust and shit of the street. . . .*
William Burroughs

LXVI.

Disabled

by seeing them touch — his head in *his* hands — put me verge of
      cry-

ing, having given them authority

over my shallow solitude. His head was borne

on the water of *his* hands. Then you appeared, a skill

of time, raising jollity

from my meatiness, the simplicity

of mutual proximity. . . .   Oh I've sworn

to and *not to* in terrible self-sufficiency ill

from perfection. . . .   The meteor shower last night showered
      misplaced

"grains of rice" (I started to write "grains of night") streaking trails
      over Healdsburg gone

California ecliptic archer to hunter trumpeted

into layered distances alone

and found me watching breathless you too watching focused there
      apex in ample solitude *un*disgraced.

Trails my summer dawn wind in other flesh strung together on scar impressions
of young Panama night. . . .

William Burroughs

LXIX.

shown
is view
of mind
which mend
by deeds
due
to kind
deity (muse?) commend
with weeds
crowned
they show
their own
grow(
th) so head confound

LXXI.

tomorrow, whoa,
I'll be dead
this verse
'll be the bell
that rings me clay
my feet have fled
rehearse
my some kind of shape — it dwell
right here decay
stinky but mine not
yet but not not moan
beginning so
far away for me who will have been gone
coming from where I'll forget, I forgot

LXXIII.

a red lamp in the green of the night rest
head on his chest be hold
tight by him on fire
or hang
from neck as lie
like vertical weight off cold
toes warming day's breath expire
where he sang
through lungs by
breathing day
go or night come strong
in silence this west-
ern shore house bed with him on long
that trail away

LXXV.

It's the sun aired for pleasure
blazing end September 95° & surf-life
spuming 15 feet sight
above us pelicans' formation shadowing the bright ground
they don't look
at us but *through* the transparent strife
of waves Once in Bolinas on 70-foot cliff top I delight-
ed to see their streaming hundreds single file migration south found
them eye to eye exactly level past me took
a look into their steady moving line prehistoric bird leather a non
flyer flying with, *that* high up, Ah day
passes plural above or below buried treasure
revealed air sea or Land's End the fog's away
today under the baring sun where nothing/no one's left alone

LXXVI.

Chill in the air — yes *that* again — proceed
as if inexorable time had pride
in its new coat (like I do: *change, season, damn you,*
change
already, I want to wear it!) or some such argument
about October and what it remembers of us. Say it takes you aside
like a new
acquaintance sexy strange
having spent
across your naked chest its first sprouty rain, the same
caress to plump your tired eyes old
from summer sun and weed-
dry, the same story of gluey love it told
you last year, liminal, wind proffering its barely-discernable name. . . .

LXXVIII.

the majesty
of his innocence or look of same was muse
to my desire compile
from it a verse
of extollation by hands & more the
penis, mmm, mightier than the pen to use
this style
of creative exploration disperse
in him from limb to limb a polysemy of attention be
full tilt hunger i.e. totally relaxed & easing
me in I'd been reading in advance
of afternoon's pleasure all eyes' work and musing on childhood fly
off page his strolling-by eyes innocence without ignorance
then he's curled-up lolling in pulling pleasure beneath my beating
    wing

LXXXV.

open
& be still
my aim's true
by which the tender target has compiled
more
than one quill
in the center of — you?
filed
my eye before
that to a point words
set aside to respect
attention for which "amen!"
& the voluminous effect
your silent squeal affords

LXXXVII.

He was swerving
toward me on that road for my possessing
though him not knowing
how to estimate
— *I* did — the charge of the encounter — *fate* did — mistaking
for casual and so releasing
what was already growing
independently, indeterminate
to his eyes but — *I* knew, making
sure to water, granting
sunlight, flatter
circumstance with psychic tropism deserving
his further attention intrigued and the matter
of the fact now finds me getting his kisses I was wanting!

XC.

Surrender or overthrow
intention by now
the last
to know as cross
self for swan-dive in spite
of woozy heights just bow
low first taste
the ground for which vertiginous loss
you might
suck luscious sorrow
out of mordant woe
and swallow it juicy like woe
grounded would you if given half a chance so
full you'll fall for tomorrow

XCI.

The best
of all possible words would skill
the poorest harper a.k.a. me
whom the magisterial force
has raised above the cost
of materials, I mean experience, which'd make me ill
if I didn't have courage to be
a wimp and give the horse
my head. It boast
on my behalf the little bearer of pleasure
in glorious guise multiplicitous who take
from heave and rest
the pulse to make
measure

XCIV.

I measured your excellence
from the beginning (& it was all about *measure)* by the way it
      snapped a smile gap-toothed where none
was thought possible sweet
in a spurt like electric show
nervy joy I could die
from that surprised delight (just twenty, not yet a poet). The hot
      stone
by which "*one takes **petal** to **rock** and **blesséd**"* was constantly there to
      meet
your urging slow
dignity
up from where the graces
speak colloquial but perform deeds
balletic of attention expense-
ive beyond counting though dressed in funky weeds
one saw rapt only their blazing faces.

for Denise Levertov

XCVI.

"How can you be redeemed?"
"If you be my witness."
"Aren't you afraid I'll betray
you?" "Everyone has his own sport."
"Can you really translate
your experience into my language?" "Less and less."
"Would you want me to take you away
from all this?" "Only as a last resort."
"What is your state
of perfect ascendance?" "To be a queen
in black and white Balenciaga with blonde hair." "What sort
of queen is that?" "The Esteemed
Re-negotiator." "Oh how can I report
on what I've seen?" "Just tell them what *I* have seen!"

IC.

while the sleepers can't stand
and fall to bed hide
under covers down, cotton, wool which is *not* despair
but smells
of the sky where a single foot hovers both
without vanity and woven from pride
here as if floating on four corners breath
makes for our sleeping ones rocking body dwells
in images only, yes, images of breath, "the free growth
of metrical laws" over-dyed
with what the eyes absorbed; death
alone separates a hand
in sleep from that awake we see
the body as a thing composed, little girl on her side curled away, will
      she wake, the
soft round shoulders and narrow waist, brown wavy hair

CII.

if you would come for days
whoever you are or seeming
to be then I'd appear
to be enveloped in our aura of intimacy now
as if in middle of night
I might turn in teeming
sheets a bough
creaking to meet the wind everywhere
so I'd under especially red flannel delight
to find your sweaty hulk like just the other day & spring
or be sprung upon flattened then that tongue
lays
bare breastbone flayed & circling down conjunctive song
I make you make me sing

CIV.

green
hand of music his orchestral beating time old
measure who correspond to who he read in letters those dial-hand
indices for sharp-eyed
witness, maker/made one, perceived
out in the cold
the fire that stand
inside — pride
wasn't, I said, *it* to one deceived
by rhetoric or argument turned
on phrases in position light unbred
in dim negotiations — "signs"; ugh — seen
rather as in *"lettres du voyant"* the glowing dead
incarnate in the mouths they've burned

CVI.

now
time
prophecies
all kinds of infirmities whites
of eyes graying or streaked with red prefiguring
that final rhyme-
word but look: after my mother's death my own plain brown eyes
turned green and gold like hers what do we know of real
       transference? knights
on their knees sing
best
when being ladies themselves ladies too have interior knights as
       knights have their knights etc. though people are also
       independently here it's clear I *am* you days
running brow
screening your pictures now all in me who praise
myself in image you expressed

CX.

Love
written on a valentine in the wind there
where the storm meets its end
for the day anyway: one twirling eucalyptus leaf. The view
is privileged towards horizon, sucked dry, daily grind
of grime and rain's rubbed it into new lucidity. Dear
friend
valentine, I mean, how new
too things seem after you've come by, confined
space opened as if truth
were best
experienced from above
like the sky might acknowledge microscopically but totally clear
        down there (here) one male breast
(mine or yours) on which a nipple stands vigilant the very sentinel
        of perennial youth.

CXI.

students are work as work has renewed
reading reading hide
study in pleasure — on the couch with Rilke drink
in images and tone — as if deeds
to a hidden country were handed out page by page an infection
of shapely mind provide
measure to think
that way: in vibrating shapes; breeds
across days correspondence or years or lives *Lorca Spicer Cocteau*
      correction
by example — admiration symmetry — a brand
of dancing partners in time and mutual sway "you
subdued
my sometime chaos *master/mistress* taking me
solidly in hand in hand"

CXIV.

where they assemble
outside of that dank bar, on the street visible together foraging social
      import, you
are seeing
them as if you weren't also streetbound abject flattery
streaming from your outstretched palm, up
from your clouded exilic eyes — true
his charcoal porkpie hat her fishnets fit the rain-slick concrete
      agreeing
with the dripping shade and din, but alchemy
has dimmer, subtler, rules: you raising golden beaten cup
of just water in this falafel diner starklit as if inner space were
      brighter — *shined in* — digest
weary the simultaneous electrification by which you read your sin
as something *they* switched on that nevertheless resemble
you, minded thoroughly of their fraternal organization, the human,
      black plastic geek glasses set, racial inequity of the serving
      stations, privilege of disposable costume, ache of age or
      youth, swirl of the oil slick coloring night, time-beat of the
      boom box, sour luxury of tahini as I watch you begin
struggle to hold up every image every node turned under radial light
      of sympathy least or best. . . .

CXV.

language things
lie
magnetic among themselves tyranny
dearer
than my best
animal presence quivering why
unfazed by total uncertainty
they see clearer
than all rest
casual accidents
so
exact voluptuous kings
grow
from non intents

CXVIII.

meet needing
as "*wailing up from blind innocence*" keen
eyed or nosed anticipate
what's coming round other bend urge
to keep lookout assured
only that it's coming your arrival unseen
by me in state
of parched antennae done purge
the crew of sickness by sleeping cured
then of craving for sweetness
lapped happily salt of sleep it's true
brine wasn't feeding
but biding kept juices ready when you
came openly needing to meet

CXX.

Hey Mark it'd be a crime
if we don't have that date now
I've seen you remembered
how it feel
to breathe into somebody hits
of smoky affinity already guessed at — so I felt with lips your short
       beard smelled bow
wow your scent recognizable & specific like a face or a name
       tendered
an offer in the air I'd surrender fixed as steel
now let's see how part fits
into part shaken
loose it was you put head on chest & called it purring waived the fee
right there stop time
4 p.m. under Monterey pines nowhere to go for a few minutes you
       & me
give or taken

CXXII.

Clearing the mist
of language in temperament one has like flowers brain
on a stem hold
together memory
and number to score
days remain
quixotic and bold
the experiment leaks toward eternity
as if more
blood were pulled from heart
than *in* the
streaming then nova subsist
of pinhole me
as stars part

CXXV.

sweet   in him   spent
large eye   canopy
down to the waist   which implied   unadorned heart
honoring
mysterious parts   not shame   from man's naked angel   free
love's man of men   eternity
tuft of   appetite   nectarine   scoop the   art
wanted ruining
about them   in his paw the
unwieldy   favor
insinuating   others on the grass   soul
now filled with   ascending scale   rent
ever   high whom my thoughts   control
in them   poured savor

CXXVI.

all my skill
all my power
even if it kill
me'll be to hour
by hour bring you intricate pleasure
as if in so show-
ing you my various or versey treasure
you might grow
fat sweet more delicious because more nourished by attention then be
freed from wrack
& wheel of this life now in rich saturation the
only promise filled before they take you back

CXXIX/CXXX/CXXXI/CXXXII.

If then mad
men make shame
it's theirs I'm stupid *and* lazy but not shamed. Who's shamed me so
that lust
is purer in the extreme
than blame?
Every fucker mounts his dog to make meaning. Forget-me-nots'
       blue haze of woe
(I forgot) parses the tree bank, old man wears bright pink to counter
       just the first glance of age: he's in! This is what I trust:
words of the dream
knotted interior, straight
lines drawn by hand. She lost him completely and it's just as well.
He had
breath like a hell-
hound but that was the bait.
The place still reeks
of person sun
anyway streams through the window and will. This is what I know:
the bed's covered in red
flannel that urges sweat the sound
of cars moving remains the sound of waves. The book's finished, the
       class is done
meeting, x is for all his words that should go
here but don't. Her head
was newly coiffed — I mean her hair — so the ground
around the chair is strewn with what she used to look like: white
as an old toenail, rare

as a viral spirochete, cheeks
like aged thunder, how else might I compare
myself to you? This is my delight:
to ride back and forth in the last subway car with my penis out
       alone
but tuned to the art
of relation. He made me swear
I wouldn't tell but the cruel
light steaming from your face
has broken all my rules. In the hand she drew a heart
that bear
the greater dignity of fire, a jewel
nailed to the forehead pulsing in place
of the heart in her hand. She shook my hand and squeezed tight.
      Behold
who's responsible for works *or* deeds;
us: we think things up, we speak or write, sing and groan.
Shalom proceeds
like water on the wind, the skiff on a beam of chance bold-
er than destiny and way farther west.
Which face will stand for the picture of me?
This solemn bearded face
with its grimace of disdain
or the slippery one gives in to the rain to retain its elasticity and
      beauty? This little heart-
shaped mouth: is that the exit-wound you favor? Which cheek
      should be
turned toward the pucker of your kiss while the mortal fever
      inflames it. Grace
to sleep from 3 to 4 p.m., grace to sleep from 12 to 8, where is your
      pain when I swallow you whole or in part

and lick my fingers? This is what I'm almost sure of: the
      construction of heaven
is wordy and black
like a very old bruise, wise, eaten, sinking from the weight of the
      east
freighted by extravagant vocabulary swollen with impulse as faded
      as a rotogravure where you're forever calling me back to
      make up for what you lack.
Watch carefully as they parcel out the invisible clouds of evening.

CXXXIV.

bind
me to your
faith take
off finger by finger will
you use
this worn funky body mine
for your sake
hold still
I forgive in advance abuse,
neglectful pride, narcissism, wait who's stripping whom? free
me
first if you'd be so kind
No? OK I'll do you: hair then skin then bones flayed free
now me

CXXXV.

O sweet vinegar millennia liberated shine
equivalent to discarding will
which it obviously is till
experience pour
the matter of connector by working inescapable lexicon store
may translated into yours still
appear composing love. Will,
consider this source gather
inheritance more
the gate ghost working smile fill
duration instrumentation vis a vis kill
occupations to equal elastic your
hand uncovering who literally will
change Orpheus to gracious

CXXXVI.

None
near.

Untold
will
be
there.

Hold   Hold.
fulfill.
              Fulfill
The   the   Fulfill
love,   love.   the
still   love
one,   Still   still.
will   one
prove.   One   One
                            will   will.
              will
              prove.   prove.   Prove.

CXXXVIII.

Air's stilled again as incipient summer does, suppressed
breathing pulls truth
out of poppies blaring just
the yellow condensation pure sun lies
in, weedy old
grass bearded not even May some youth
sprouting trust
all subtleties
of ardor extended. . . . told
then a story about when I'll be young
tomorrow, hawk on cypress branch squawking at me
by best
perchable fallen log, scotch broom yellow too, perfumed the still air
          as time itself be
speaking tongue. . . .

CXLI.

Claudio, Steffano, Salo, Jésus, Christian, Holger, Dirk, alone
without you my somber eyes
can
note
the
empty, well, platonic form in front of 'em & then despise
the man
or men I dote
on, fictive, no, not you. For you I'd be
myself again if you would be yourselves, delighted
in your loveliness, really, imagination's form so fine in real-time, gain
of human countenance the gaze I found in you, on you, or you in
        me, prone
before each mirroring eyes sprayed out acknowledgment as beauty
        kindly given, sweet, pain
only of the threshold tested, crossed, hushed, tense, into, *invited*. . . .

CXLII.

friends walk; bones begin to creak; wild iris and dandelion; bay leaf
      scented air; each rents
body for mere seasons; lunch on kalamata olives, smoked turkey,
      hummus; hate
to hear those
bones creak; old friends defer to time loving
walking measure; slanted redwood shade; golden poppies splatter
      hills; who'd have foreseen this kind of elegiac afternoon the
casual alternation of rain and sun a state
of how it grows
and falls proving
exactly one's situation small between material forces and what
      pushes back; "be
steady" the poem said; this is what your
eyes are permitted to see, this may hide
beneath resplendent ornaments;
cracked boulders in shallow stream glaze orange; red walking dust,
      browned mud; nothing noticed will be denied:
all mine

CXLVI.

Grand entrance or exit diva-worthy arms outspread end
to end charting, what?, earth-
wide the one that got away a loss
this big or in fabulous array
display the full store-
house of meaning no dearth
of acquisition from Agamemnon gold to Nixon dross
top to bottom bedecked bewigged bedewed bedazzled like
       authoritative gay
life live to sensation more
orifice than focus especially given AIDS-acknowledged short lease
mortal ignition of bliss encompass spectrum not spectral men
spend
men material strewed being totally incarnate head to toe then
wash themselves in glorious spewed excess.

CXLVII.

One wants love and assuaged desire, one wants the hair-breadth
       spine of foxtails, the sprouty droop of rattlesnake grass,
       shuffling whirr of the blue jay's thick flight, metallic hoot of
       the *koukouvaya* owl predawn Crete still heat no other sound
       except
small lap of the Libyan Sea. . . . One gets these and murder in
       the first degree for killing an administrator, shit pile for
       shoeshine, spare change for square foot, grainy lust of the 2
       a.m. bar impenetrable hide bound, the dead letters in their
       special nowhere office, the dead air quiet, still. . . .
One wants a first person tighter than betrayal, or a plural shiftier
       than signage, one needs spectator heels for walking now
       to balance the hump of shoulder or finds pennies on the
       sidewalk to place over eyes, take care! . . .
One sees as if through tinted lenses elegant continuance and
       perforating dis-ease,
hallucinogenic pine trees and swallows in loopy unrest. . . .
One calls out the names of the days and the years, Febu-ember,
       Haveyouever, Jewels and Mai-Lai, Year of the Fox Kittens,
       Year of the Stuffed Gorge, Year of the Cream Patina,
       Sloughed Skin Year, Lapping Dog Year, Year of Bitterns and
       Mice — ill-
met again by moonlight but happy to cast a shadow. . . . By the
       plum tree rounding out in purple leaves, with a light wind
       reminiscent of secret-hero-of-the-poem, plangent as
       magnolia but quicker to recede, one questions which are
the letters that make sense and which ones are dispensable, which is
       the thud of the one true monosyllable, please,

which one gives vent to a solitary moan and which expressed

the will of the people — and *which* people? words are frangible,
      pliable, pitiable dust but oh what traces they leave! One
      longs for specificity in abstraction, presence in absence, love-

in-idleness, the magic of translucence and the skeletal superiority of
      fact. . . . The spasms of bright

light show what's there then not there, there then not there, the
      perch of his just-fallen hair over brow, sharp wag of Puggy's
      tail, Mary's first pinafore, Rusty's erection, Steve's freckled
      nose, a Texan trout rumored to be gigantic but never rising
      kept

hidden by the tangle of submerged branches, June bugs, swamp mist
      on Lake Cherokee 1958, stars drawling constellations over a
      hay-ride one tries to remember but memory won't be tried. . . .
      One hears in the close night

rumors of cars, rumors of people, rumors of gunshots, champagne
      corks, tra-la-la-ing, obsessive argumentation, squeak of the
      ol' mattress spring, gurgle of Gallo hastily slurped, slam of
      the front door solid oak, siren far off then near then far off,
      one listens carefully, dutifully, calibrating as if to repudiate or
      approve. . . .

CL.

rain rain exceeds
temper for (formerly) fair May might
scream "no more!"
under sway
of wet wet how hate
no sun in sight
and no you! a bore
limpy day
hollow state
shell ill-
fitting oh hear me
stumble, Love, deeds
deeds not words the
missing skill

CLI.

reason
upended is
measure the
beat beat love
takes pride
in a Miss
Thing yells "you go girl" she be
out to prove
nothing inside
or out be trai-
psing & trailing her train call
it treason
to logic she say spinning let fall
what may

CLII.

I'm going going lost
to time body's losing it I can tell stiffer looser goodbye sworn
off supple maneuvers evidently some kindness
needed to temper its creak swearing
does no good here I go hairier less hair constancy
left only for evanescence torn
from time and *its* hoary blindness
light as air bearing
ultimate gifts of a shrug and a feint see
I
used to be the
most
everything upon whom soon enough the
very least'll lie!

CLIII.

Sun might be the cure
or sex might, or falling fast asleep
where sun slants onto bed late afternoon San Francisco June your
       back fired
into being for me who's found
it spread there, iconic, breast
calmed by such flagrant proximity, the rise in you steep
as any possible fall. If I desired
more the ground
would be too big to cover; you then be guest
upon whom roiling face of love
lies
singular. To endure
further's some other symmetry: steady eyes
on steady eyes will prove.

CLIV.

Disarmed
by chance while asleep
so that the staged dream had all the appurtenances of a world made by
hand — I mean the brand
of locality was everywhere: Norma's posture, Kevin's 35 millimeter
      lips, potted orchid squeezing out the last flush of color, path
      in the park slick with Sunday dew, perpetual
thread of the time-keep-
ing rhyme. . . . Attention's the remedy
for what it attends, hand
raised in salute or the *adios* wave, thrall
of pure syntax contiguity face to face on fire
to prove
each line warmed
by particulars fore and aft. Love
's the art imagined by desire.

INVOLUNTARY LYRICS: A Foot Note

The line is dead; long live the line!

After fifteen years of prose poems I was wondering a way back to verse. The End of the Line I had envisioned — surfeit of the Projective's obsession with lineation — started reviving. I was missing a torque one feels in the body of thought.

Orders are delivered: Each "Involuntary Lyric" ends its lines with the same words as a correspondingly numbered Shakespeare sonnet — though these rhyme-words have been shuffled out of sequence to spring their traps (to *unring* the sonnet.) With these moored but mutated determinants the lines turn on a hinge (sometimes there's just the hinge), projective only in the sense of being shot toward Shakespeare's word already waiting there. A new measure is unloosed — vertiginous but restrained — within these fixations.

Poetic constraints quicken me, foils to my florid sensibility and voluptuary lexicon. An art like S&M, perhaps (which isn't my art of eros) where boundaries pressure the interior that cooks. Vanilla S&M? — maybe, since there's plenty of play against the rigor here, with swinging indeterminate line-lengths, and wide-open topical windows.

Windows privilege the daily; I wanted "involuntary" to include what experience was doing to me. Composure disrobes: hilarity or severity. The quotidian acts as a given, just as Shakespeare's language is given to the poem. Not to be coy (Elizabethan as it may be) but it makes *attention* my mistress (OK, he's in drag.) Ballasted by the end-words poem to poem, the *Lyrics* fuse incursions from the left hand to the fixed but floating stations of the right. Alternating modes high or low, meditative or notational, they attempt to balance what's being given: the measure of attention. The *tension* of attention.

If divination is suggested, one is raised by language as one raises it. Theme? Age is in my hand I find, and love-called-desire rouses its own cognitive prosody. They play on me, poor fool or master, poor Puck, little cup of mortality. I couldn't announce a theme to which I didn't become subject.

I was happy to invite back in to my poems names and places [hello, friends] and let my own contradictions find their voices. Though I didn't *read* the *Sonnets* for *Involuntary Lyrics* — their semantic weight being much too powerful and me far too suggestible — interplay was inevitable: didn't erotics bleed right through, with so much incidence of direct address and all those cruisy "eyes"? Still, I've relished contemporary circumstance among the strictures and structures, so the Renaissance's "little death" happens vertical in a park as well as the romantic boudoir. Doubling syntax, popping rhyme and fine unfashionable abstractions are similarly evoked, scions to the shameless exuberant Elizabethan vocabulary or shadows of its rhetoric.

If I've been fearless in maneuvering this territory it's because Shakespeare's *Sonnets* are in the tradition so fundamental as to be almost transparent, merged with their process and moment which are elementary, elemental. They're primal material, almost as pure as the flowering language itself — in this case, I might say, as pure as Form.

A.S.

INDEX OF FIRST LINES

Aaron Shurin is the author of over a dozen books of poetry and prose, most recently *The Paradise of Forms: Selected Poems,* one of *Publishers Weekly's* Best Books of 1999, and *A Door* (2000). His honors include fellowships from the National Endowment for the Arts, the California Arts Council, and the San Francisco Arts Commission. Since 1999 he has co-directed the Master of Fine Arts in Writing Program at the University of San Francisco.

INITIATIVE

Omnidawn Publishing is committed to preserving ancient
forests and natural resources. We elected to print *Involuntary
Lyrics* on 50% post consumer recycled paper, processed chlo-
rine free. As a result, for this printing, we have saved:

2 trees (40' tall and 6-8" diameter)
986 gallons of water
398 kilowatt hours of electricity
109 pounds of solid waste
214 pounds of greenhouse gases

Omnidawn Publishing made this paper choice because our
printer, Thomson-Shore, Inc., is a member of Green Press
Initiative, a nonprofit program dedicated to supporting au-
thors, publishers, and suppliers in their efforts to reduce their
use of fiber obtained from endangered forests.

For more information, visit www.greenpressinitiative.org

Library of Congress Cataloging-in-Publication Data

Shurin, Aaron, 1947-
  Involuntary lyrics / Aaron Shurin.
    p. cm.
  Includes index.
  ISBN-13: 978-1-890650-23-0 (acid-free paper)
  ISBN-10: 1-890650-23-4 (acid-free paper)
  I. Title.
  PS3569.H86I585 2005
  811'.54--dc22

                                    2005014884